Map It!

Contents

Elspeth Leacock

Places

Maps are drawings that show how places look from above. If you go to Washington, D.C., a map can help you find your way to the White House.

Washington, D.C.

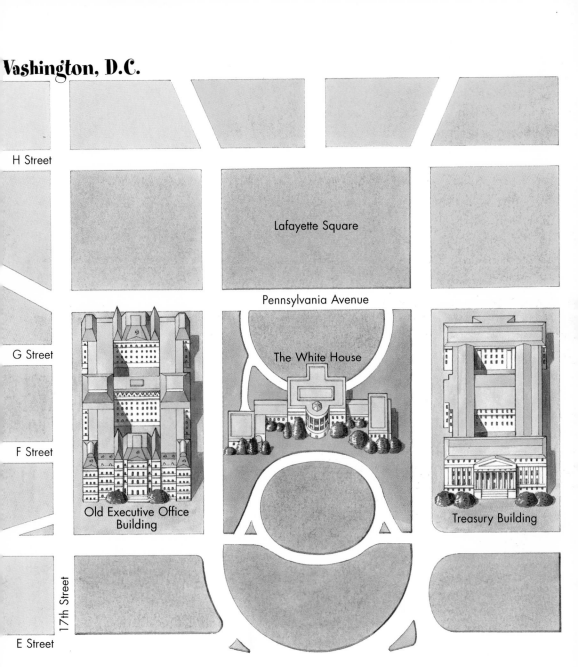

H Street

Lafayette Square

Pennsylvania Avenue

G Street

The White House

F Street

Old Executive Office
Building

Treasury Building

17th Street

E Street

How can you tell which building is the White House?

Symbols

This map uses pictures with labels to show where things are. Can you find the Statue of Liberty?

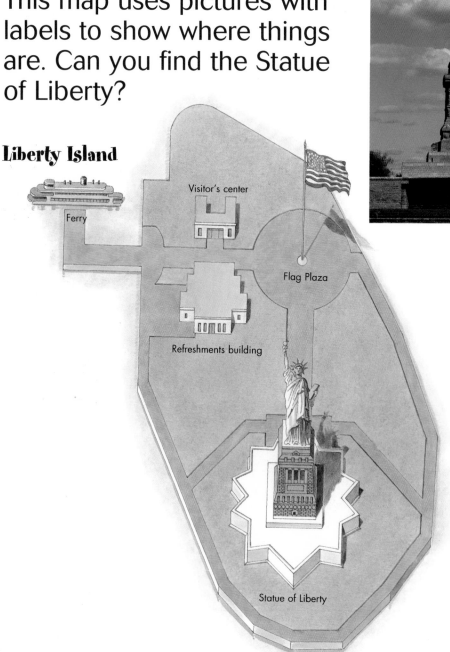

Liberty Island

Ferry

Visitor's center

Flag Plaza

Refreshments building

Statue of Liberty

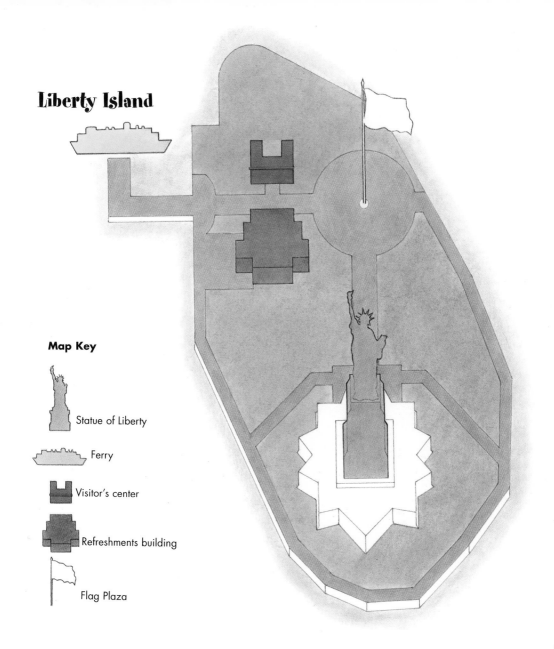

Liberty Island

Map Key

Statue of Liberty

Ferry

Visitor's center

Refreshments building

Flag Plaza

This map uses **symbols** to show where things are. Use the **map key** to discover what each symbol stands for.

Directions

The words *north*, *south*, *east*, and *west* tell **directions** on Earth. When you face toward the North Pole, south is behind you. Is west to your right or left?

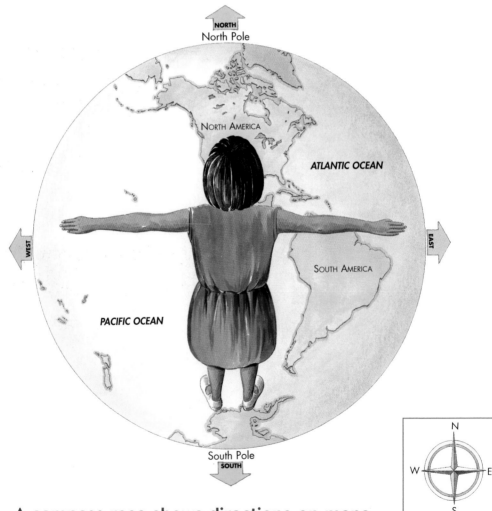

A compass rose shows directions on maps.

Sacramento, California

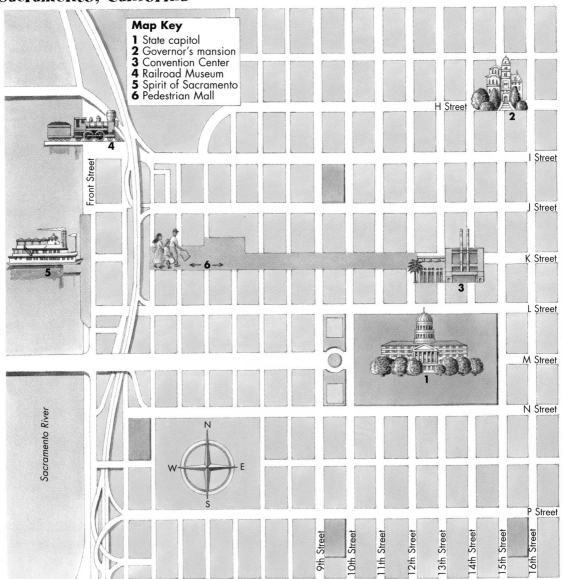

Map Key
1 State capitol
2 Governor's mansion
3 Convention Center
4 Railroad Museum
5 Spirit of Sacramento
6 Pedestrian Mall

H Street
I Street
J Street
K Street
L Street
M Street
N Street
P Street

Front Street

Sacramento River

9th Street
10th Street
11th Street
12th Street
13th Street
14th Street
15th Street
16th Street

If you stand on the corner of 13th Street and N Street, what building will you see to the north of you?

Landforms

Texas is a big state with many **landforms**. Maps can use symbols to show these landforms.

A mountain is a great mass of rock and earth much higher than the land around it.

A river is a large stream of water that flows on the earth.

A lake is water surrounded by land, like a very large puddle.

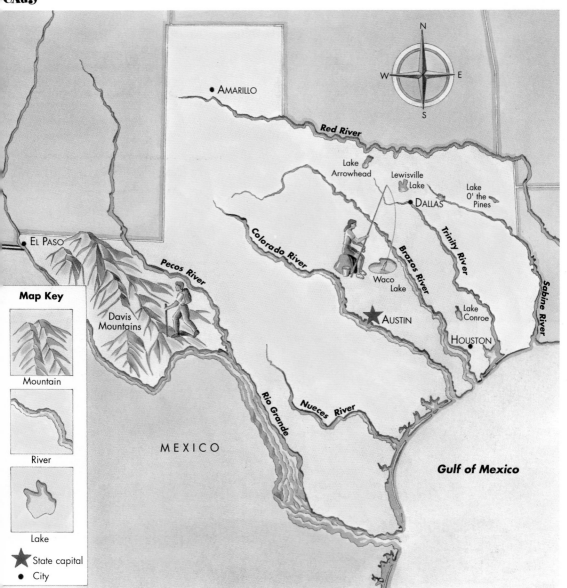

Map Key

Mountain

River

Lake

★ State capital
● City

Mountains are fun to climb. To climb a mountain, would you go to east or west Texas? Use the map to find which way to go.

Transportation

There are many places to see in Florida, and there are many ways to go. Road maps use symbols to show different ways to travel.

Florida

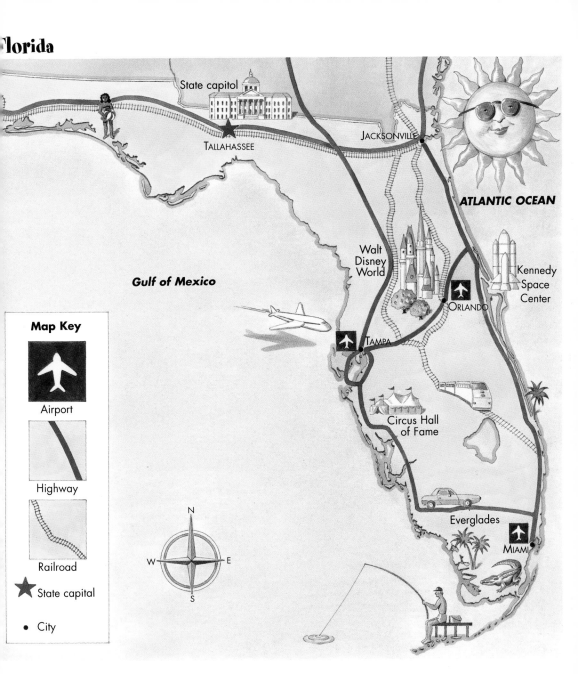

State capitol

TALLAHASSEE

JACKSONVILLE

ATLANTIC OCEAN

Gulf of Mexico

Walt Disney World

ORLANDO

Kennedy Space Center

TAMPA

Circus Hall of Fame

Everglades

MIAMI

Map Key

Airport

Highway

Railroad

State capital

City

N
W   E
S

What place would you like to visit in Florida?
How can you travel there?

Boundaries

The United States is one country made up of 50 states. On the map you can see each state's **boundaries**, or borders.

The United States

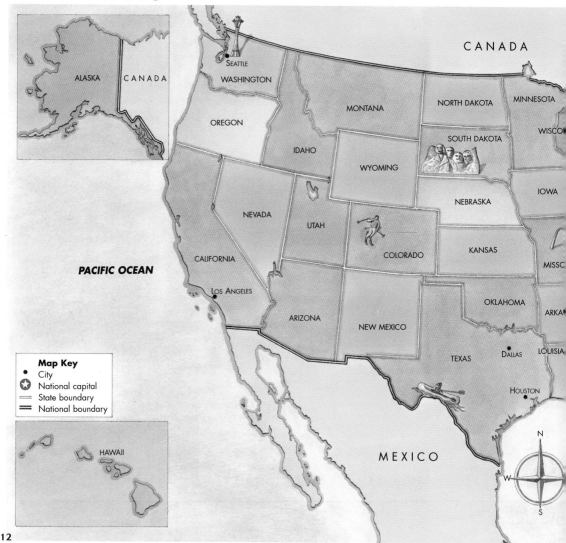

Map Key
- • City
- ⭐ National capital
- ═ State boundary
- ═ National boundary

ALASKA   CANADA

SEATTLE
WASHINGTON
OREGON
IDAHO
MONTANA
WYOMING
NEVADA
UTAH
CALIFORNIA
LOS ANGELES
ARIZONA
NEW MEXICO
COLORADO
KANSAS
NEBRASKA
SOUTH DAKOTA
NORTH DAKOTA
MINNESOTA
WISCO
IOWA
MISSO
OKLAHOMA
ARKA
TEXAS
DALLAS
LOUISIA
HOUSTON

PACIFIC OCEAN

CANADA

MEXICO

HAWAII

N
W   E
S

This map shows our national boundary too.
What country is our neighbor to the south?

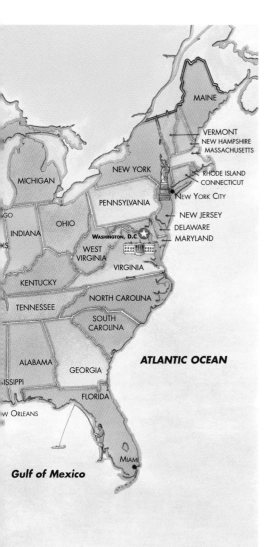

Boundaries are drawn on maps, but they are not drawn on Earth.

The World

This map shows Earth's seven **continents** and four **oceans**. Around the middle of Earth there is a line called the **equator**.

The World

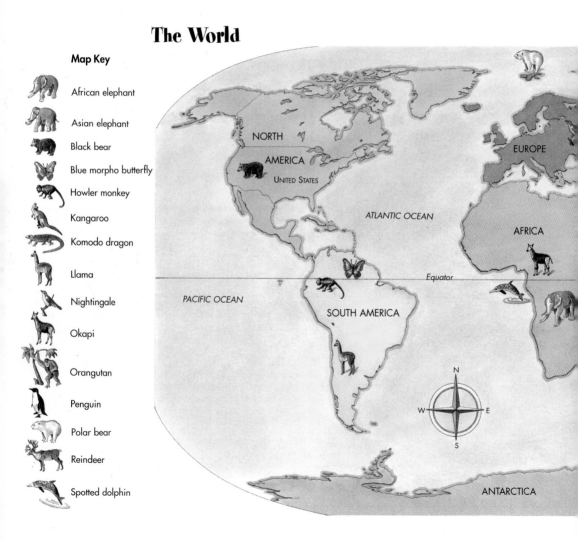

Map Key

- African elephant
- Asian elephant
- Black bear
- Blue morpho butterfly
- Howler monkey
- Kangaroo
- Komodo dragon
- Llama
- Nightingale
- Okapi
- Orangutan
- Penguin
- Polar bear
- Reindeer
- Spotted dolphin

NORTH AMERICA

UNITED STATES

EUROPE

ATLANTIC OCEAN

AFRICA

Equator

PACIFIC OCEAN

SOUTH AMERICA

N
W   E
S

ANTARCTICA

14

Places near the equator can be very hot.
Places far from the equator can be very cold.
What animals live near the equator?

The equator is drawn on maps,
but it is not drawn on Earth.

A Key to Maps

What does each of these map symbols stand for? For help you can look back at the pages where you learned about them.

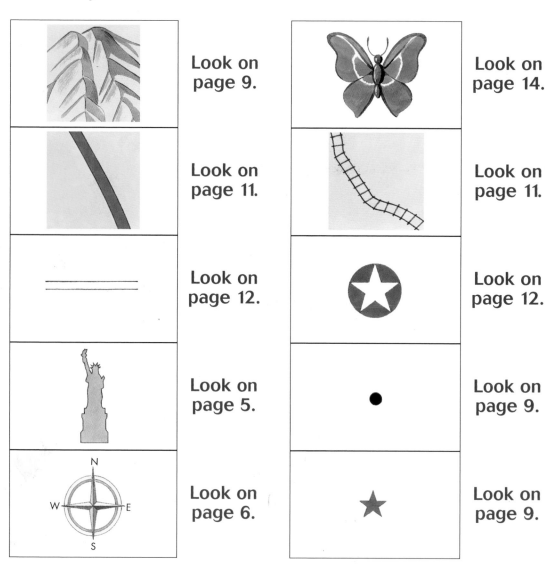

Look on page 9.

Look on page 14.

Look on page 11.

Look on page 11.

Look on page 12.

Look on page 12.

Look on page 5.

Look on page 9.

Look on page 6.

Look on page 9.